FIFTH EDITION—TWO HUNDRED & FIFTIETH THOUSAND

WORK AND WAGES;

OR, THE

PENNY EMIGRANT'S GUIDE

TO THE

UNITED STATES AND CANADA,

FOR

FEMALE SERVANTS, LABORERS, MECHANICS, FARMERS, &c.

CONTAINING

A short description of those countries, and most suitable places for Settlement; Rates of Wages, Board and Lodging, House Rent, Price of Land, Money matters, &c.; together with full information about the preparations necessary for the voyage, instructions on Landing, and expenses of Travelling in America. With an Appendix.

BY VERE FOSTER.

LONDON:—W. & F. G. CASH, 5, BISHOPSGATE WITHOUT;

MANCHESTER, HEYWOOD; NORWICH, J. DARKEN; NEWCASTLE, BARKAS; LIVERPOOL, SHEPHERD; GLASGOW, GALLIE & SONS; EDINBURGH, MENZIES; DUBLIN, M'GLASHAN, MASON; YORK, J. BROWN; BRISTOL, W. H. COOK; BIRMINGHAM, WHITE & PIKE.

AND ALL BOOKSELLERS.

Price One Penny each; or Tenpence per dozen.

AS I WAS.

REFERENCES FOR ADVICE AND INFORMATION.

LIVERPOOL AND ALL OTHER BRITISH PORTS.— The Government Emigration Officer, whose office in Liverpool is at foot of Bath Street.

QUEBEC, MONTREAL OR TORONTO.—The same.

BOSTON.—Irish Emigrant Society, 4, Congress Square.

NEW YORK.—St. Catherine's Convent, Houston Street, near Broadway; British Emigrant Society, 86, Greenwich Street; Office of the Commissioners of Emigration, Anthony Street, Broadway; American and Foreign Emigrant Protective Society, 27, Greenwich Street.—(The Society's circular will be forwarded free, on receipt of a stamped envelope, by their Agent, E. JONES, 45, Union Street, Liverpool.)

ST. LOUIS.—Irish Emigrant Society, Chestnut Street.

A Dollar is equal to 4s. 2d. sterling, being composed of 100 cents., each of which exactly equals a halfpenny.

Much expense may be saved at New York, or other port of arrival, by purchasing a Through Ticket, instead of paying for each conveyance separately.

[SEE COVER AT END.]

[*Price One Penn.*

WORK AND WAGES.

"Emigration has been latterly carried on, so far as the Irish are concerned, ALMOST ENTIRELY, if not quite so, by remittances from those who have previously emigrated, and no doubt the PRACTICAL proof which these remittances afford of the prosperity of those who make them has contributed in no slight degree to stimulate whatever disposition might exist towards emigration. The amount of those remittances, so far as we could ascertain them, are stated in former reports, but we have no hesitation in here reproducing an account which affords so honourable a testimony to the self-denial and affectionate disposition of a whole people. The accounts returned to us as remitted, or prepaid for passages to America, were, in 1848, upwards of 460,000*l.*; in 1849, 540,000*l.*; in 1850, 957,000*l.*; in 1851, 990,000*l.*; in 1852, 1,404,000*l.*; in 1853, 1,439,000*l.* We need scarcely repeat that these accounts show only the sums remitted through the principal banks and mercantile houses, and that we have no means of ascertaining the amount (probably very large) sent home through private channels."—*Government Commissioners of Emigration,* 1854.

WHILE the soil of Great Britain and Ireland is so monstrously monopolized in large pieces by a few thousand families, and the laws so impede its sale during the life of the owner, or its division at his death, as to render it almost impossible for the actual tiller of the soil to become possessor of a single acre of land in his own native country; while such is the overcrowded state of the population, and the excessive competition for employment, that there are in the United Kingdom one million of paupers, and millions of almost paupers, whose daily life is but a succession of privations and misery, and a mere struggle for existence; while in a so-called Christian country many thousands of young men find times so hard that they are tempted by the offer of free board and lodging, and the pay of a few pence per day, to hire themselves out for a term of years as butchers, not of pigs and cattle, but of young men of other nations who have been driven to enlist by a similar cause;—it is a comfort to know that there are, in other quarters of the world, accessible at the expense of a very few pounds, immense countries, rich in abundance of fertile soil, and so vast in extent as to be incapable of being monopolized for many generations yet to come. Several, at least half a dozen, of these countries contain many tracts of land, each larger than England, and each as yet without a single inhabitant, except a few savages and many hundred thousands of buffaloes or wild cattle, whose meat I have known to be in such overabundance in South America that it could not be sold in the country, and would only fetch a halfpenny a pound in the towns. In their more settled districts, they are so thinly inhabited that farmers, railway contractors, builders, and other employers of labour, are seriously inconvenienced by the impossibility of obtaining at any cost the services of a sufficient number of domestic servants, labourers, and mechanics.

The following information about North America (containing only two of those countries) for the use of intending Emigrants, and of persons wishing to know how they may lay out their spare money so as permanently to better the condition of the poor of the United Kingdom, is derived from my own personal experience and observation. It is offered to the public in this cheap form, in fact, as must be evident, at the bare expense of publication and sale agency, to supply the want of a cheap guide, which, I believe, is felt, there being nothing of the kind published at a less price than sixpence, and that out of date. I earnestly hope that it may be useful in contributing to raise the wages, and otherwise better the condition of the working classes in this country, at least in a few districts,—of some who get very low wages, or who have not steady work, or who, though receiving good regular wages, feel much anxiety of mind about the prospects of their children, by directing their removal to a country where they will be better paid, and where there is no need of such anxiety; and of others by relieving them from that excessive competition for employment which is one of the principal causes of existing poverty and misery, and which, I fear, is about to be aggravated by stoppage of trade and increase of taxes in consequence of the brutal war which the leading so-called Christian nations are now carrying on with their utmost energies, and which is a sad burlesque on their religious professions and on the main precepts of their gospel.

In order to fit myself in some degree to give the following instructions, I have twice crossed the ocean as a steerage passenger, first in the packet ship Washington,* from Liverpool to New York, carrying 934 passengers in the winter of 1850-1; and the second time in the Canadian screw steamer Cleopatra, from Liverpool to

* The Diary of my voyage was printed by order of the House of Commons (Paper 198, 1851).

Quebec in the autumn of 1854, and have twice travelled many thousands of miles throughout a great part of the United States and Canada. I have given away 250,000 copies of previous editions of this tract, but I am unwilling any longer to impose on the good-nature of the many friends, of whom the principal were my present publishers, who have kindly assisted me in their circulation, and I cannot afford to continue, without return, the great expenses of printing and advertising.

THE UNITED STATES.

EXTENT.—The Republic of the United States of America, formerly a colony of Great Britain, from which its independence was finally established in the year 1783, when its extent was not one-third of what it is now, and its population was about three millions, is bounded E. and W. by the Atlantic and Pacific Oceans, S. by the Gulf of Mexico, and N. by British America. Its greatest length from E. to W. is about 2,500 miles, and its greatest breadth from N. to S. about 1,450 miles. It contains 2,963,666 square miles of land, or, in other words, is more than ninety-five times as large as Ireland, more than sixty times as big as England, and is more extensive than any other country in the world, except the Russian, British, and Chinese empires. It is composed of thirty-one independent States, and nine territories (see cover). If peopled as thickly as England it would contain more than a million of millions of people—that is, more than the present population of the whole earth. A great deal more than two-thirds of this vast country, fourteen hundred millions of acres of land, belongs to the Government, and is for sale; so you see it is no empty boast of brother Jonathan that he has land enough to give every man a farm. POPULATION—According to the census of 1850, besides wild Indians, 23,191,876; and is supposed to have increased since by births, and by emigration from Europe and from China, so as to be now equal to the population of the United Kingdom, namely, 27½ millions, including over 400,000 Indians. There is, therefore, a population of about nine persons on an average to each square mile, while in England there are 332. CITIES.—New York, having 800,000 inhabitants, is exceeded in population by two cities only in the world (London and Paris), and Philadelphia by eight only, exclusive of those in China and Japan, whose population is unknown. RAILROADS.—There were last year, 1854, 17,317 miles of railroad in use, and 12,526 being constructed, or more than as much of either in all other quarters of the globe put together.

CANADA.

EXTENT.—The province of Canada, formerly a colony of France, was ceded to Great Britain in 1763, when its population was but little over 65,000 inhabitants. It is composed of E. and W. Canada, the latter being best suited for settlement by emigrants on account of its milder climate and more fertile soil. Canada is bounded N. and E. by British possessions, S. and W. by the United States. Its greatest length from E. to W. is about 1400 miles, and its breadth from N. to S. scarcely exceeds 100 miles. It is twice the size of the United Kingdom. POPULATION, in 1852, 1,842,205 inhabitants. RAILROADS in use Dec. 18, 1854, 760 miles; being constructed, 1,183 miles.

THE BEST PARTS OF AMERICA TO GO TO.

United States—Western States of Ohio, Indiana, Michigan, Illinois, Wisconsin, Iowa, and Missouri, and western parts of New York and Pennsylvania. In all these States railroads and other public works are being carried on extensively. *Canada.*—North shore of Lake Ontario, and the peninsula between lakes Ontario, Erie, and Huron.

WAGES.

Persons having constant employment at fair wages in this country, and having no children, would be more contented, I think, by stopping where they are.

The usual wages throughout the United States for servant girls are from 4 to 8 dollars (usually 5 or 6, and in the Western States 6 or 7) per month, and full board, with liberty to wash for themselves. In East Canada the wages vary from 2 to 6 dollars (see Money, p. 8); in West Canada 3 to 6 (usually 4, and seldom 6). Good female cooks may after no long time, in large hotels or private houses, get as much as 12 dollars, or if good pastrycooks, or professional cooks, 16 to 20, or 24 dollars per month. Women who can milk cows, and churn and bake, are much sought after. The wages of farm labourers in both the United States and Canada, in addition to board, lodging, and washing, vary from 8 to 18 dollars per month, the year round; the usual wages for a middling hand being about 12 dollars, and in the State of Illinois, which is settling and thriving fast, and where labour is very scarce, 15 dollars per month. Newly-arrived emigrants, men or women, being unknown and unused to the ways of the country, and therefore requiring to be taught their business, must not expect the lowest of the wages here mentioned for the first week, or perhaps month; and if arriving in winter, will scarcely get anything in the Eastern cities, and should not listen to the interested advice of lodging-house keepers, who, for the sake of getting their custom for a few days longer, will tell them that the wages offered are too low. On the contrary, they should readily accept an offer at almost any wages, show what they are able to do, get used to the ways of the country; then, but not till then, ask to have their wages raised, and if refused, go. Throughout the spring and summer they will find no difficulty in getting other places. Labourers engaged during the summer, say for three months only, should get from 12 to 26 dollars per month, and board, according to what they can do. Harvest labourers paid by the day receive from $1 to $1 75, and board (see Money, p. 8). Those paid by task-work will get from 50 to 75 cents per acre, according to weight of crop, for cutting wheat with the cradle scythe: an anyway good cradler will cut about 2⅓ acres per day. Boys 12 to 14 years of age will get from farmers $3 to $8 per month, and board. Girls of same age from 75 cents to $1. The usual daily wages on public works throughout all parts of the United States and West Canada, are one dollar a day, and in some places $1 25 in summer, and from 3s. to 3s. 6d. sterling in winter. I believe it will be far better for a labourer to seek employment with a farmer rather than on public works. On the latter he may be uncomfortably lodged in a rude log or board-house, the cold and rain coming in through the openings between the boards, and may often be making roads through sickly swamps, exposed to chills, and fevers, and other sickness; eating inferior food, and perhaps surrounded by brawling companions who have no fellow-feeling for one another, and whose God is their whiskey. If sick, there will be no one to tend him, as his fellow-labourers must be out at their work all day: but in a farmer's house he will be more likely to be well fed and lodged, and to keep his health, and, should he be sick, he will probably meet kind women to nurse him; he will not have to shift so much from place to place when one job is ended to seek another; he will be earning wages regularly every day, wet or dry, and, though he may receive less, I believe he will be able to save more, with which he may in 2 or 3 years buy out and out, and stock a farm of 100 acres or more. Sempstresses get in the United States and in Canada from 25 cents to $1 per day, or about $1 50 per week, with board; without board, $3 per week. The usual wages of other persons are—

	WEST CANADA.		UNITED STATES.	
	Range.	Most usual.	Range.	Most usual.
Carpenters ..	$1 37 to $2	$1 75	$1 50 to $2 50	East .. $1 50 / West.. $1 75
Masons or Bricklayers	$1 75 to $2 50	$2 25	$1 50 to $2 50	$2 00
Blacksmiths .	$1 50 to $2 00	$1 50	$1 00 to $2 50	$1 50
Printers	1s. to 1s. 4d. per 1000 ems, or about $8 per week.		25 to 35 cents per 1000 ems on newspapers: make $10 to $12 per week.	
Hotel Waiters	$10 to $14 and $20.		$12 to $14 and $20.	

Tailors, I was told, would have more comfort in England with constant employment, but less anxiety of mind in America about the prospects of their children.

Bootmakers, I was told, could make about half as much more in West Canada and the Western States than in England. There is abundance of work in the cities, and there are plenty of openings for becoming landowners in the country, which makes a constant drain from the one to the other, leaving continual openings for new comers. There are also plenty of opportunities of acquiring city lots, and, as a general rule, bootmakers do acquire property.

Clerks and shopmen, unless experienced bookkeepers, will not, I believe, generally succeed. Professional persons may expect much difficulty. Teachers will be welcome in the Western States to board and lodging, which will be a help to them while looking for some more suitable situation, but they will receive very little pay. I believe the most suitable part for them is West Canada, where very much attention is now being paid to education, and where school salaries can be readily added to by means of private tuition of an evening.

BOARD AND LODGING.

Board and Lodging, which ranged till last year from $1 25 to $3 per week, is scarcely anywhere less than $2 25 per week, and is generally $2 50 or $3. For women, 50 cents less. It will probably be lower again next year, in country districts especially.

HOUSE RENT in the outskirts of Towns and in Villages.

United States.—One room and a kitchen $2 50 to $4 or $5 a month, usually $3 50 or $4. Two rooms and a kitchen, $4 to $6. *West Canada.*—One room and a kitchen, from $3 to $4 or $5. Two rooms and a kitchen usually $3 50 or $4. A small house, rented by the year, $4 to $5, or $6 per month.

PRICE OF LAND.

The fixed price for Government land in the United States, after having been once offered for sale at auction, when mill sites, &c., are bought up by speculators, is $1 25, except near some railroads assisted by Government, when it is $2 50 per acre. By a recent law reducing the price of public lands to actual settlers, all public lands which have been offered for sale for ten years and remain unsold, are priced at $1 per acre; for fifteen years, 75 cents; twenty years, 50 cents; twenty-five years, 25 cents; and for thirty years, 12½ cents. These lands are to be found in the Western States of Illinois, Wisconsin, Iowa, &c., and are good, but have remained unsold because far from markets or timber. Railroads, however, are rapidly approaching, and curing these evils. Nearly all the public lands east of the Mississippi, whether in the United States or Canada, are either entirely covered with forest (as in West Canada and the State of Michigan), the labour of clearing off which is almost enough to drive a new settler crazy, unaccustomed as he is to handle the axe, or else are entirely destitute of timber, as in the States of Illinois and the southern part of the State of Wisconsin. In order to find *public* lands for sale at the Government price, which have a judicious mixture of timber and pasture, it is necessary to go, I believe, either to the northern part of the State of Wisconsin, north of the Fox and Wisconsin Rivers, or west of the Mississippi River into the State of Iowa, or the territory of Minnesota; but timber land adjoining the above public lands can be generally bought from *private* owners at an advanced price of from $5 to $10 or $15 an acre.

There is no Government land remaining for sale in the better part of West Canada, except in a small Peninsula containing half a million of acres, between Lake Huron and the Georgian Bay, just obtained by treaty from the Indians, and which is about to be offered for sale at auction, probably in 200 acre lots, and will be no doubt all sold within this year. A common price of unimproved farm-land bought of a private owner in the Western States, five or six miles from a village or small town, is from $2 50 to $15 per acre, according to situation; and of land partly cultivated and fenced, and provided with a house, $10 to $20 per acre. I would strongly recommend any one intending to buy land to see it first, and satisfy himself that it is good, as there is much trickery on this subject, especially on the part of Land Companies in England; and it is as likely as not that land bought in England, as is thought very cheap, turns out to be a sickly swamp or barren sand, or a grand extent of rock, or otherwise worthless, and dear at a penny per acre. He should see, too, that water is handy, and a school, and should avoid the neighbourhood of rivers as well as marshes, where chills and fevers invariably prevail. It would be well even for a farmer, with a good deal of capital, to lodge himself and family, and to work with some intelligent old settler for a month or two, or a year, before he sets up for himself, so as to learn the ways of the country by practice, observation, and conversation, thus saving himself some very costly experience. It is a common custom in many parts of the country for a new settler to rent a farm at one-third of the produce, or, if furnished with cattle, implements, and seeds, at one-half.

Whether to take Shipping for New York or what other Port.

Vessels sail frequently for America from Liverpool, London, Glasgow, Dublin, Cork, Limerick, and occasionally from other ports—to Quebec, Boston, New York, Philadelphia, Baltimore, Charleston, and New Orleans.

The advantages of sailing for Quebec or New Orleans are the cheapness of passage across the ocean, and the great facility, at a very cheap rate, for persons and baggage, of reaching far distant points, especially from New Orleans, without change of conveyance. The emigrant is less subject to ill-treatment on board ship to Quebec, and obtains redress more readily there than elsewhere. The time to sail for Quebec is from 1st April to 1st August; to New Orleans between the end of September and middle of March: but it is advisable to avoid going by way of New Orleans, even perhaps in the depth of winter, as it is a very unhealthy place.

The advantages of sailing to Boston, New York, or Philadelphia, over Quebec, are, that the voyage is much shorter and safer for sailing vessels than up the intricate channel of the Gulf of St. Lawrence, and the ships are less crowded, the American laws requiring more space than British laws. The passage to Boston is usually more expensive by about 10s. than to any other port, and the journey from Boston into the interior has also been about 10s. or 12s. 6d. more expensive; but the treatment in ships bound to Boston is by far the best, and so, with exception of Quebec, has been their treatment on arrival by Government officers or by Societies.

The advantages of going to New York are, the quickest passage, except to Boston, a more abundant choice of the best ships, and the great variety of railway and other communications from thence into the interior. On the other hand, my opinion is, that passengers are more liable to be imposed upon as to both the quantity and the quality of the ship's provisions in vessels bound to New York, and are more subject to gross imposition and robbery, without any probability of redress, at New York than at any other port.

Philadelphia and Baltimore are the most convenient ports from which to reach the western parts of Pennsylvania and Virginia, and the borders of the Ohio river.

"Those bound to Boston, New York, or Philadelphia, should endeavour to land in March, April, or May," as observed to me by Horace Greeley, editor of the New York Tribune, "as near the first of May as possible. After that time farmers have engaged their help for the season, the climate grows relaxing to European constitutions, and labour is with more difficulty obtained. Of course, those who have means or reliable friends to help them to work, can land almost any time, but those who come later than the first of October must expect a hard winter." Work is very scarce in the Northern States and in Canada in winter; also travelling into the interior is then extremely expensive, as the lakes, rivers, and canals are frozen; and, there being no competition of steamboats, railway fares are higher.

COST OF PASSAGE.

The price of passage from Liverpool to the different America ports varies very much, being generally highest in April and May, and lowest in midwinter and just before harvest. If ships are scarce and emigrants numerous the price of passage rises daily; if, on the contrary, there are plenty of ships and emigrants are scarce, the price of passage falls as the day of sailing advances, which is a principal reason why passengers in the same ship pay different prices. In the spring especially the sooner a passage is engaged the better, as emigration is most brisk at that time. The following is the range of the lowest prices from Liverpool to

	£ s. d.	£ s. d.	Average Length of Passage.*
Quebec (usually under £4)	3 0 0	to 5 0 0	46¼ days
Boston (usually between £4 and £5)....	4 0 0	„ 5 10 0	41¼ „
New York do.	3 0 0	„ 5 10 0	37 „
Philadelphia do.	3 5 0	„ 4 10 0	44¾ „
New Orleans (usually nearer £3 than £4)	3 0 0	„ 4 0 0	52½ „

Passengers to the United States under fourteen and over one year of age pay 10s. less; to Quebec half price. Infants 10s. each to the United States, but free to Quebec. These differences arise from the difference between the laws of the United States and those of Great Britain and Canada; the former requiring the same space in ships but only half rations for every passenger over twelve months

* Taken from a list of 530 ships which sailed from Liverpool between Nov. 1853, and Nov. 1854.

old, and imposing an importation tax varying at the principal ports from 8s. 4d. to 10s. 6d. on each passenger, not excepting infants, whereas the British law requires only half of both space and rations for passengers between one and fourteen years of age, and nothing for infants, and the Canadian law imposes only 4s. sterling importation tax on passengers over fourteen years of age, 3s. on those between one and fourteen years of age, and nothing on infants. This tax is in all cases included in the passage money. From London to the United States the fares are usually about £1 or £1 10s. higher than from Liverpool; children from one to fourteen years of age paying half the charge for older persons.

Screw steamers took passengers last year from Liverpool to Quebec for £8 8s. including a sufficiency of cooked provisions. I went in one, and neither took nor needed any extra provisions, except half a dozen eggs. I would recommend, however, a ham and some *butter* and cheese, sweet preserves and fresh bread, as adding much to comfort. Other steamers took steerage passengers from Liverpool to Philadelphia, and from Glasgow to New York, for £9 9s. and £8 8s.; but all of these steamers have been diverted from their regular trade to America, being engaged in carrying troops to a worse place, where they will make but a bloody reputation, add nothing to the comfort of their families, as they would be able to do in America, and from which I fear most of them will never return.

Lunatics, deaf, dumb, blind, lame, or aged persons, poor women with children and without husbands, or any persons likely to become a public charge, will scarcely be taken at all to the United States unless giving security that they will not be chargeable for support within five years after arrival. Canada is more hospitable, so they can sail for Quebec.

PREPARATIONS NECESSARY FOR THE VOYAGE.

AT LIVERPOOL.—On your arrival at Liverpool or other port of departure, go straight to your lodging-house, if you have chosen one; if not, go at once to the office where your passage is engaged, or where you wish to engage it, and find out when the ship will sail, where it is, when you should go on board, and when the berths (sleeping places) will be marked, and take care to be on board at that time, and to get the number of your berth marked on your passage ticket. At many of the offices there is a store where baggage will be taken care of free of charge.

Lodging.—The usual charge for lodging, including use of kitchen fire and cooking utensils, and storing of luggage, is from 4d. to 9d. per night—4d. being a very common price. Children under fourteen years of age are usually charged less, according to agreement; infants nothing. Mind you make an agreement beforehand.

Choice of a Ship.—Choose a ship that is well ventilated—that is to say, go in a ship which has one sleeping deck for passengers rather than two; be careful that you can not only walk upright on this deck, but that it is at least seven feet from the deck above, as is the case in all the liners, and that the ship has not a great deal of housing on the outside deck to interfere with a proper current of air below. See that the ship has high bulwarks (wooden walls), at least six feet high, at the side of the outside deck, so as to protect passengers from being drenched every time they come on deck by the spray, whenever the sea is a little rough. If you have a family choose a ship, if possible, which has separate water closets for males and females, and if possible one of these below, or else at the hindmost end of the vessel on deck; if below, then take with you some chloride of lime got from a chemist, and throw a little into the closet now and then, to stop bad smells.

The weak among my readers—and I would add the very poor but that they cannot afford to choose—should be careful, if possible, to select a ship in which they are not required to cook for themselves, but are engaged to be supplied daily with enough of cooked provisions. To the richer passengers who can bribe the cooks with a half crown now and then, to pretty women who can coax them with their smiles, or to strong men who can elbow their way with their broad shoulders, such advice is not necessary, as they can have access to the crowded cookhouse at any time, and any number of times daily; but the others have often to wait for hours in the wet, or even all day, to cook a single meal, and the caprice of the cook seldom allows them even then to get a meal properly cooked. They are pushed off to make way for others till the time allowed for cooking is over, or a storm rises to prevent it. The want of properly cooked food especially, and of proper ventilation, are I believe the principal causes of diarrhœa, dysentery, typhus fever, and cholera on board ship.

How to Engage your Passage.—At Liverpool, or any other port of embarkation for America, be careful whom you employ to show you to a shipping office; ask no questions in the street, pay no attention to the offers of service of any one you meet, not even to ask your way to any place or office, as each such question may cost you five or ten shillings or more; but, having gone on board a number of ships and chosen the one you like best, buy your ticket yourself at the head agency office of the ship, the address of which will be posted up in very large letters on board the ship itself; or, what will be better still, ask the person to whom you may have been recommended from home to get the ticket for you. You will then be more sure of being charged the market rate of passage. He will probably get it cheaper for you than what you could get it for yourself, and yet make a few shillings for himself in doing so. When you go to a shipping office or to a shop to make purchases be sure to go quite alone, as if any person shows you in or goes in with you it will most likely be to get his commission in one way or another out of an increased price to be charged to you. All the offices and shops pay commissions of from five to seven and a half per cent., or more, to persons who bring them customers, and the worse the ship the higher the commission; it is therefore the interest of persons of no character to induce emigrants to go in as bad a ship, and pay as high a price for their passage as possible. When you have got your ticket mind you keep it, giving it up to no one except for a moment to the Government officer who will visit the ship to inspect the passengers just before you sail, and who will tear off a piece of every ticket, which serves him as a note of how many passengers there are on board, their ages, and so on. Keep the ticket till *after* the end of the voyage as long as you like, as the law allows, in order that you may at all times know your rights, and as an evidence of your agreement in case of your having to seek redress.

Emigrants should on no account, except when properly recommended, suffer themselves to be so misguided as to pay in Europe their passage any further than to the port of arrival of their ship in America, as it often happens that railroad or other tickets bought in Liverpool are found to be of no use in America, and the fare has to be paid over again, and no redress can be got in America for breach of an agreement made in England. This especially applies to agreements about baggage. Of course there are honest persons in this trade as in others, and much expense and imposition at New York may be saved by buying tickets from such persons, who may be heard of by inquiring of the Gov.^t Emigration officer at each port, or of me at Wimbledon, Surrey. It must be clearly understood that any recommendation given by me one year or month will not be good for another, unless renewed.

Sea Stores.—The quantities of ship's provisions which each passenger fourteen years of age gets, or rather is entitled to, without extra payment on the voyage to America, are as follows :—

BRITISH LAW.		AMERICAN LAW.	
3 quarts of water, daily		3 quarts of water, daily	
2½ lbs. of bread or biscuit	weekly	2½ lbs. navy bread	weekly
1 lb. wheaten flour	,,	1 lb. wheaten flour	,,
5 lbs. oatmeal	,,	6 lbs. oatmeal	,,
2 lbs. rice	,,	1 lb. of salt pork (free from bone)	,,
½ lb. sugar	,,	½ lb. sugar	,,
2 oz. tea, or 4 oz. cocoa or coffee	,,	2 oz. tea	,,
2 oz. salt	,,	8 oz. molasses and vinegar	,,

According to the British law, a passenger over one and under fourteen years of age gets only half allowance; according to the American law, every passenger over one year old gets full allowance. Of course passengers will get fed according to one scale or the other, not both. The British law provides that certain substitutions may be made at the option of the master of the ship for the oatmeal and rice, and very properly requires that these provisions should be given to the passengers daily, in a cooked state, but this is not attended to one time in a hundred. Each passenger is entitled, by law, to lodging and provisions on board from the day appointed for sailing in his ticket, or else to 1s. for every day of detention, and the same for forty-eight hours after arrival in America. As regards extra provisions, they must depend on taste and circumstances. As much as heretofore will not be required if the ship's provisions shall be issued cooked according to law. In my voyage in the "Washington," from Liverpool to New York, which occupied thirty-seven days,

I took the following extra provisions, which I found sufficient, and which were the same in quality and quantity as I had been in the habit of supplying previously to passengers whom I had assisted to emigrate to America :—1¼ stone wheaten flour, 6 lbs. bacon, 2¼ lbs. butter, a 4 lb. loaf *hard baked*, ¼ lb. tea, 2 lbs. brown sugar, salt, soap, baking powder. These extra provisions cost 10s. 6d. ; I consider them to be plenty, so far as necessary articles are concerned. A ham, a cheese, more *butter*, more flour, some potatoes and onions, and in case of children, many little extras, such as sweet preserves, suet, raisins, preserved milk, treacle, lemons, &c., would be palatable and desirable additions, particularly during the first fortnight, until the stomach gets inured to the motion of the ship. *Remember*, that you cannot, when at sea, run to a shop to get what you want ; you must get it beforehand. I also took the following articles for the use of myself and messmate, the prices of which, of the commonest kind, but quite good enough for so temporary a purpose, should be as follows, according to size for one, two, or more persons :—Tin water-can, 6d., 1s., 1s. 2d. ; tin hook saucepan or boiler, 5d., 7d., 10d. ; frying-pan, 6d., 8d., 10d., 1s., 1s. 4d. ; tin dish or wash-basin, 5d., 6d., 9d. ; tin kettle, 8d., 1s., 1s. 4d. ; tin tea-pot or coffee-pot, 6d., 8d., 10d., 1s. ; tin plate, deep, so as not to spill easy, 1½d., 2½d., 3d. ; tin pint mug, 1½d. ; chamber vessel, 6d. ; knife, fork, and spoon, 4½d. ; treacle-can for 3 lbs. or 6 lbs., 4d., 6d. ; barrel and padlock to hold provisions, 1s. to 1s. 3d. ; small calico bags to hold ship's weekly flour, oatmeal, rice, biscuits, tea and sugar; towels and rubbers ; straw mattrass, length 5 ft. 10 in., 8d. to 1s. 2d. (a better description of do. would cost 1s. 4d. to 2s. 4d.) ; blanket for one person, 2s., or, according to size, per pair, 4s., 6s. 6d., 9s. ; rug, 1s., 1s. 4d., 1s. 6d., 1s. 10d. ; sheets, each, 9¼d. Instead of buying a mattrass, it would be better to bring an empty tick from home and fill it with straw at Liverpool or other port. A crock will be wanted for the butter, price, holding 3 lb., 3d. Bring some epsom salts or pills, or other purging medicine with you, and plenty of treacle for children, as rolling in bed and want of occupation during the voyage stops digestion. Families would do well to take with them a tin slop pail, price 1s. 6d. to 1s. 10d., or japanned, 2s. ; also a broom and small shovel. The handles and spouts of all tin articles should be riveted on as well as soldered. The bottoms of trunks should have a couple of strips of wood nailed on to them lengthwise, one at the front edge and the other at the back edge, to keep them off the damp floor. *See that you get all the articles of sea stores which you pay for.* Almost any sort of clothes will do for the voyage, dirt, grease, tar, and salt water will spoil anything good.

Baggage.—The enormous quantity of unnecessary baggage frequently brought by emigrants causes a heavy expense and a world of trouble, costing them perhaps their value several times over before they get to their journey's end, a very small quantity of baggage being allowed free of charge on railroads, and extra baggage being charged most extravagantly high to make up for the lowness of passenger fares ; besides, there is imposition in cartage and porterage at every stage. Most articles of clothing are as cheap in America as in England ; anything woollen, however, and strong boots, may be taken with advantage (shoes may be laughed out of use, especially with plates and nails which heat the feet, and are not necessary in so dry a climate and on such stoneless roads). Carpenters should bring their light tools, but heavy tools will not be worth the expense of carriage. Pins, tape, needles and thread should be brought, as they take up little room, and are extremely dear in America. Not many dresses or bonnets should be brought, as the difference of their style from those worn in America may cause them to be laughed out of use, and the money paid for them will have been wasted. All clothing and other baggage not wanted on the voyage should be packed in separate boxes, with the owner's name clearly marked on them.

MONEY.

The best shape in which emigrants can take small sums of money to America is in English gold and silver, which will pass as readily in America as in England, but cannot be changed in England without loss. It will be most safely carried on the person. British bank notes are not current in America, and will not, I find, be readily exchanged by bankers because of the risk of sending them by post. On account of the risk of loss on the voyage by robbery or other accident, it is better for a passenger to pay any amount he may have over, say £10 or £20, into a well-known bank, taking a certificate of deposit, or a draft on an American bank, in exchange. Assisted emigrants should be provided with means to be paid to them on *arrival in America*, through a banker or the agent of the ship, to enable them to go up the country in search of employment. When an emigrant *pays* gold in America, he should insist, until he gets acquainted with the different bank notes, on *receiving* his change in gold or silver, or he may find himself in possession of worthless bank notes, American banks being very liable to fail. The following table will show the United States and Canadian values of English money :—

English Coins.	U. S. Value. Dollars.	Cents.	Canadian Value. Shillings.	Pence		English Coins.	U. S. Value. Dollars.	Cents.	Canadian Value. Shillings.	Pence
A sovereign is worth	4	84	or 24	4		Shilling		23 ,,	1	3
Half-sovereign	2	42	,, 12	2		Sixpence		11 ,,		7½
Crown	1	20	,, 6	1		Fourpence		7 ,,		5
Half-crown		60	,, 3	1½		Threepence		5 ,,		3½
Florin		46	,, 2	6						

A sovereign is generally worth about 4 dollars and 84 cents, sometimes 2 or 3 cents more or less ; so, for any amount under £1, it is near enough to calculate a cent and a halfpenny as exactly equal. A dollar is composed of a hundred cents, each equal to a halfpenny, and is written thus—$1 ; a dollar and a half, and a dollar and a quarter, thus—$1 50, $1 25. There is no Canadian coin, yet payments are calculated in Canadian value, which is puzzling.

Last thing.—The last thing to do before going on board is to get a few loaves of fresh bread *hard baked*, and a good-sized piece of roasted or boiled fresh meat to eat when cold. An emigrant's guide which I have seen contains the following sound advice :—" When the time arrives to go on board ship, do so without delay, not allowing yourself to be persuaded by the lodging-house keeper to sleep on shore, as there will be plenty of time in the morning. Such an indulgence has cost many the loss of a passage and a week's delay in Liverpool.

" Go on board your ship, if possible, before it moves out of the dock, rather than after it has gone into the river, as in the latter case you may have to stop for hours in the rain on the pier head waiting for the small steamer which is to take you alongside the ship, and getting your luggage, and provisions, and bedding, for which and yourself there is no shelter, soused and spoiled with the wet, or else have to hire a small boat to take you to the ship at an enormous expense. Whether you go in the steamer or in a small boat you will have to get on board in a very scrambling manner, and your baggage may get all knocked to pieces, as often happens. For the cartage or porterage of your baggage from your lodging to your ship, make a clear agreement beforehand with the carter or porter as to what you are to pay, and let that agreement include the carrying of your baggage not only board the ship, but ALONGSIDE OF YOUR BERTH. From the moment your luggage gets on board take care that it be well watched ; and if you lie in the ship in dock a night, keep a close guard over it, as ships are at such times infested by thieves, who cannot be known from passengers," and whom the officers of the ship are otherwise too busy to look after.

THE VOYAGE.

The berths (sleeping places) are each from six to six and a half feet long, and eighteen inches wide, ranged one over the other in double shelves along the side of the ship. Single men are berthed separately from the rest of the passengers. All clothing and other baggage not wanted at sea should be put out of the way till the end of the voyage, as the officers of the ship may direct. Passengers should be particularly cleanly on board a crowded ship to prevent ship fever from breaking out (this is very important), and should keep much on deck to breathe the fresh air for the same reason, and pay a cheerful obedience to the discipline of the ship. The floor should be sprinkled with vinegar sometimes to sweeten the air, and chloride of lime should be sprinkled now and then in the water-closet, if any, between decks. Be careful of your sea stores, as your passage may be longer than you expect, and it is better to have some over at the end than be short at sea.

How EMIGRANTS MAY SECURE GOOD TREATMENT FOR FUTURE PASSENGERS, MORE EFFECTUALLY THAN CAN BE DONE BY ACTS OF PARLIAMENT, whose regulations are easily evaded.—Whenever it happens, as is sometimes the case, that passengers have received the full allowance of provisions of good quality for which they have agreed and paid, and have been otherwise very well treated during the voyage, they should, in justice to the captain or other officers, before leaving the ship, express their thanks to them in a written address, have it published in the newspaper where they land, (for which no charge will in general be made,) and then post a few copies of those papers to the principal papers in the old country; and the same if they have been very ill treated.

ON ARRIVAL IN AMERICA.

Do not listen to any one of the numerous persons who will come on board the ship, or meet you as you go ashore, saying that they are the agents of the Government, or of this or that benevolent society, or of a railroad or steamboat company, or telling you that the person you are asking for is dead, or the office is closed, and the owners bankrupt; but, as at Liverpool, ask your way in a respectable shop to the place you wish to go to. If you are not bound to any particular house, or railroad, or steamboat, one of you, if a party, should look about for a lodging, while the rest mind the baggage on board. Be on your guard against extortionate charges for cartage, board and lodging, contrary even to agreement, against the purchase of false travelling tickets, or payment of extravagant prices for the conveyance of yourselves and *baggage* into the interior.

In selecting a lodging-house, be careful not only to find out beforehand what you will have to pay, having it expressly understood that there is to be no *further charge* for *storing your luggage*, but get a printed card of prices, and make your payments daily, at least for the first day or two, in dollars and cents. What is called a shilling in New York is worth only sixpence sterling. A shilling, sterling, is worth 1s. 3d. of Canada money. The lowest expense at emigrant lodging-houses in New York is 50 cents for three meals and bed, or from 12½ cents to 18¾ cents for a single meal or bed. In a better kind of house the charge is $1 a day, or 25 cents a single meal or bed. Fruits and green vegetables should be eaten sparingly for some time after landing, and river water should not be drunk excepting boiled as tea, coffee, &c., for fear of diarrhœa. Emigrants should leave the overcrowded cities on the sea coast as soon as possible and go up the country, the further the better, and, leaving the main lines of travel, where emigrants are in each other's way, scatter right and left, inquiring for work on any terms. The propensity of emigrants to remain about large cities, and especially those on the sea coast, is very much complained of by Americans, and with too much foundation. There they land at the rate of a thousand or more daily throughout the year; many of these loiter days, weeks, and months, wasting their money and idling away their precious time, quietly waiting for Providence to turn up something for them, until their last penny is spent, their trunks are retained by the lodging-house keepers to pay their bills, and they are turned out beggars on the streets. Meanwhile, a few hundred miles up the country throughout the spring and summer they are badly wanted, and might at such times, if common labourers, be earning 4s. 2d. sterling a day, boarding themselves, or if good harvesters, even as much as 8s. 4d. sterling, besides their board. They should not stickle for high wages at first, when their abilities are not known, but care more to learn during the first month how to earn high wages afterwards.

TRAVELLING IN AMERICA.

There are four principal routes into the interior from New York, as follows:—

1. From foot of Cortlandt-street, by steamboat up the Hudson river, 145 miles, to Albany; from A. by railroad, 298 miles, to Buffalo on Lake Erie; from B. by steamboat, 305 miles, to Detroit, Michigan; from D. by railroad, 278 miles, to Chicago, Illinois; from C. by canal, 100 miles, to Lasalle on the river Illinois; from L. by steamboat, 307 miles, to St. Louis in the State of Missouri. By paying a few dollars more, passengers can travel by railroad all the way by this and all the other routes.

2. From foot of Duane-street, by New York and Erie Railroad, 460 miles, to Dunkirk on Lake Erie; from D. by steamboat to Toledo; from T. by railroad, 247 miles, to Chicago, and so on. From Chicago there are railroads in many directions.

3. From pier No. 1, North River, by steamboat, 27 miles, to South Amboy; from S. A. by railroad, 63 miles, to Philadelphia; from P. by railroad, 353 miles, to Pittsburgh, on the Ohio river; from P. by steamer, 485 miles, or by railroad, 360 miles, to Cincinnati, and so on by steamer to Louisville and St. Louis, or by railroad to Chicago. There is sometimes not water enough for steamboats, on the Ohio, between Pittsburgh and Cincinnati. This should be learned before leaving New York.

4. From New York, as above, to Philadelphia; from P. by steamboat and railroad, about 100 miles, to Baltimore; from B. by railroad, 380 miles, to Wheeling, on

the river Ohio; from W. by steamboat 391 miles, or by railroad — miles, to Cincinnati. This route between Baltimore and Cincinnati will very soon be shortened — miles, by crossing the river at Parkersburgh, 102 miles below Wheeling. Passage by canal costs much less, but is so slow that there is no saving expense.

The fares for 1855 on all these routes from New York, will be $10 to Cincinnati, $11 to Chicago; 50 lbs. of baggage being allowed free, and $2 25 charged for every 100 lbs. of extra baggage to Cincinnati, $2 50 to Chicago, and fares for less distances in proportion. The fare by Route No. 2, to Dunkirk, Buffalo, or Niagara Falls, will be $6 or $5 50, and the charges for extra baggage $1 per 100 lbs.; on Route No. 4, the fare from Baltimore will be to Cumberland, 180 miles, $2 50; Wheeling, 379 miles, $3 75; Columbus, 514 miles, $5 25; Cincinnati, 770 miles, $5 25; Louisville, 912 miles, $6;—100 lbs. baggage being allowed free, and $1 being charged per 100 lbs. extra to Wheeling; $1 75 to Cincinnati. The fare from New York to Philadelphia last year was $1 50; to Baltimore, $3 or $3 50; to Albany, 25 to 50 cents, or by railroad $1; to Boston, $2 50; to Montreal, Toronto, or Hamilton, $6. For fares from New Orleans, see letter of the British Consul in the Appendix. From Quebec to the West:—

Conveyance.	Miles.	Fare. (sterling.) s. d.		Conveyance.	Miles.	Fare. (sterling.) s. d.
*Montreal,	steamer....180....	3 0		London,	railroad....666....	23 9
*Kingston,	„ ....369....	11 0		*Windsor,	ferry ....776....	23 9
Toronto,	„ ....547....	19 0		*Detroit,	railroad....776....	27 0
*Hamilton,	„ ....590....	19 0		Chicago,	„ ..1054....	35 0

Passengers change conveyances at the places marked (*). Baggage 100 lbs. free. From Quebec to Boston, railroad, 26s.; to New York, railroad and steamer, 19s. In the U. S. and Canada, Children under 12 years half price, and under 3 free.

My application for information about routes and fares in Canada and the United States, for 1855, have not been answered, excepting by the Superintendent of the Baltimore and Ohio, New York and Erie, and Hudson River Railroad as above, otherwise it was my intention to publish full tables of each route.

Intoxicating drinks are very cheap in America, and there, as elsewhere, an over-indulgence in them is the greatest curse to the labouring man, and the main obstacle in the way of bettering his condition, depriving him of his wits, character, and self-respect, and shutting him out from respectable employment. As no liquors are to be got on the voyage, he will then have an opportunity of breaking himself into total abstinence from their use except in cases of sickness, thus economizing his hard-earned means, to be more satisfactory and less selfishly employed in adding to the comforts of his family, and providing for the education of his children.

Many a reform is wanting in the mode of conveying emigrants from Europe to America. For instance, shelter ought to be provided for deck passengers on board of steamers plying between Irish and English ports. It seems to me perfectly disgraceful and inhuman, that, whether in summer or winter, wet or dry weather, by day or night—and these steamers cross the channel invariably by night—while horses are comfortably boxed up, there is no shelter whatever from the inclemency of the weather, (and what a winter we have had!) for men, women or children, who often, in consequence, contract serious illness or perish. Passengers are not so treated in American coasting steamers. (2.) Shelter ought to be provided on the pier-head at Liverpool, for the many thousands of emigrants who have frequently to wait with their baggage for many hours in the rain for the steamer which has to take them alongside of their ship, in the river. (3.) The baggage of passengers ought, as is done with merchandize, to be shipped from the dock wall, or even from the ticket office, and to be lowered alongside of their berths at the expense of the parties connected with the ship, by whom it can be done at one twentieth of the usual cost to an emigrant. (4.) A sufficiency of cooked provisions ought to be served out to the passengers daily, as is the case on board the Canadian screw steamers. (5.) Water-closets should be provided for female passengers either between decks or at the stern of the vessel. (6.) The American import duty on *poor* emigrants seeking to better their condition, ought to be abolished. What would be thought of the justice of levying an equal amount of *poor's-rate* from the poorest as from the richest classes of society? Besides, the owners of city property in America are immensely benefited by this immigration.

As some of my readers may have been lately cautioned by those who wish to check emigration, against emigrating *at all* to America, on account of the *distress* in its overcrowded *Eastern Cities* this winter from over speculation and bankruptcies as eighteen years ago, and universal short crops, and a partial stoppage of trade caused by the European war; for the reassurance of such persons, I have extracted from the *New York Daily Times*, of January 20, 1855, some important information which will be found in the Appendix.

Other persons may have been cautioned against emigrating to America on account of the political prejudice which has been growing there of late against foreigners, and more especially against Irish Catholics, on account of a numerous faction who have nicknamed themselves *Know-nothings*, seemingly, because, like upholders of slavery, they know nothing of true republican principles, since they profess in the same breath entire civil and religious liberty, and uncompromising hostility to Roman Catholics. Should immigration to the United States receive any material check, these people would soon be brought to their senses, since railway and highway contractors, builders, farmers, and other employers of labour, though the most arrantly bigoted know-nothings, can hardly get on without a supply of labourers, mechanics, and domestic servants, whose industry is the foundation of their fortunes, as well as of those of New York shipowners and owners of city property, &c.

They will therefore be interested in inviting as much as possible, instead of checking immigration to their shores, putting up with its few drawbacks for the sake of its great benefit. The know-nothing movement may be looked upon as a passing gust of popular bigotry, provoked by injudicious conduct on the part of many foreigners, showing its strength in the ballot box, but not in deeds of violence, and not interfering with the prospects of the working classes, and honourably opposed by much of the most respectable and popular press in America; for instance, the *New York Times*, and *Tribune*, which, with the *Herald*, have the largest circulation.

In conclusion, I am anxious to repeat that, in my opinion, the apprehension of a more general war in Europe, and consequently of more stoppage of trade and employment, and of increased taxation and distress in this country, which are already beginning to be felt, render it more especially desirable that the poorer classes of this country should emigrate *now*, for the sake of all who are dear to them, and whom they would wish to shield from future suffering. Emigration lotteries might, I think, be instituted with great advantage, as a more effectual means of raising wages, and otherwise bettering the condition of the working classes, than strikes, or any probable parliamentary reform.

APPENDIX.

From W. Chambers, Editor of the Edinburgh Journal, to V. Foster:—" The enclosed (3rd edition) appears to me a very useful detail of particulars."

Extract of Letter from Horace Greeley, Editor of the New York Tribune, the most popular American Weekly Newspaper, to V. F., Sept. 4, 1854:—

" I can find no essential errors in your little tract (3rd edition). Let emigrants be careful to buy no tickets of irresponsible persons, no matter how cheaply offered, but procure their passage always under the advice of some of the disinterested authorities to which you very properly refer them. If they cannot read, let them have their tickets and receipts carefully read over to them by some trusty friend, so as to be sure not merely that they are honestly dealt by, but that they clearly understand the engagement, and do not expect what has not been promised them. Many emigrants mistake in their eagerness to get as far west as possible. I believe most efficient labourers can do as well near this city as elsewhere, provided they land here at the right season, say from the 20th March to the 10th May. At that season almost any cleanly, civil, industrious man, can find work as a gardener's assistant or farm labourer, in the State of Connecticut or New Jersey, or the river counties of our own State, all within five hours ride of this city. If reduced to a few shillings when he lands, let the emigrant swing his frock over his shoulder, and walk two or three days journey in any landward direction, and he will find work. . . . . If he is single, or has but a small helpful family, I think this is his preferable course. If he has a swarm of young children let him push west, if possible—land, food, and shelter being cheaper in the newly-settled districts. . . . ·

Entreat all who come over to leave our cities at the earliest moment, to shun crowds and fights, and grog-shops, and theological wranglings, and attend strictly to their own business. I hope we shall pass the Maine liquor law this winter, that will probably bring these shameful feuds to a termination."

From W. H. Mure, British Consul at New Orleans, to V. F., Dec. 8, 1854:—

"On a careful examination of your tract (4th edition), I can see no alterations or important additions to suggest..... The prices of deck passage to the different ports on the Mississippi are from $3 to $5, the latter price to Louisville and Cincinnati: the amount of baggage to these two last-named places is sometimes limited to 100 lbs. when the river is low, with a charge of 50 cents per cwt. for all above that amount; to all other places there is no charge for extra baggage."

From P. H. Finigan, Farmer, near Joliet, Will County, Illinois, Nov. 2, 1854:—

".... Good household servants, capable of all manner of housework, can in any part of the State of Illinois get without difficulty from $1 00 to $1 25 per week; that is, $4 to $5 per month. Many get more, but that is the average rate. Labourers on public works never get less than 87½ cents per day, nor more than $1 25, except masons, who can at any time get $1 50, and sometimes $2 per day. Labourers on farms are in this State largely sought for, and can always get an agreement for a year at $15 and $18 per month, with board and washing; and in haying and harvesting time we are very glad to get men at $1 and $1 25 per day. Even boys of twelve and fourteen years old in this State have no difficulty in finding places at $8 and $12 per month and board, through the summer months.

"While on this head I may as well answer your sixth question, *viz.* 'Price of farms ten or twelve miles from market.' I live on a prairie, which, for agricultural purposes, cannot be surpassed—level as a lawn, without a stone, and here and there small groves of timber. Well, all around here unimproved lands can be bought at $6 and $8 per acre, in lots of 80, 160, or 320 acres, all the Congress lands have been taken up here; but farther west and south there is still a large quantity which may be had for $1 25 per acre. Here timber is scarce, and consequently dear; it is worth from $30 to $50 per acre, but so good that five acres will fence 320, and give a family firewood for life. My farm is ten miles from market, and cost four years ago but $250.... I think that for emigrants coming to this country with a small capital, and with a knowledge of farming, Illinois is the best State in the union. Living for labourers is here as cheap as anywhere; labourers in the towns and cities can get good board for $2 dollars per week; or if with a family, can rent a house of two or three rooms for $2 to $2½ per week. I have now given you all the information of the correctness of which I can be certain."

*Extract from the New York Daily Times of January 20, 1855:—*Mr. F. L. Olmsted, a gentleman residing near New York city, interested in agricultural investigations, has addressed, through the newspapers, a circular to the farmers of the country, calling for information about wages of labour and demand for hired workmen, their cost of board, kind of food, and chances of becoming landowners and employers of labour in their turn. His replies have come from nineteen different States (out of thirty-one), and eighty-eight different persons. These replies show strikingly the just now important fact, that while the *seaboard* cities are full of unemployed and depressed labourers, the farmers, even in the comparatively immediate neighbourhood, cannot obtain the necessary help to carry on their operations. Common sense then seems to say, Give not soup, but railway tickets to your unemployed. It appears that the average rate of wages for an intelligent farm hand, when engaged by the year, is $136 50, besides board; or $13 50 per month, and board, when employed in the summer months only, by which has been generally understood the term of *eight months* of active farm operations; when hired by the day, 75 cents per day and board. The highest wages given are $240 a year in Iowa, $230 in Michigan, and $220 in Illinois. The highest in the Northern States is in Connecticut, $180; the lowest is in Maryland, $80, and New York, $85 to $100. To the questions in regard to food, the usual feeling expressed in the replies is, that any questions should be asked. One from Missouri writes, "In the West food is no object, especially the substantials, and every man gets what will fill his stomach, and if he does not it is his own fault; and when they do not have beef or pork, there is generally, he says, plenty of fish, poultry, bacon, dried beef, and venison." All promise food in abundance. A farmer in Iowa states, that *four-fifths* of the labourers employed in his village are now owners of land. A correspondent from Missouri writes, "One or two years' service are sufficient to procure money to buy 80 or 160 acres of Government land, or to purchase a town lot and erect a house thereon; or to get a horse and dray, a yoke of oxen and wagon, buy land and set up farming." Another, that it is "inevitable" for the labourers to become landed proprietors; others dilate on the point and give multiplied instances in their own neighbourhood and experience. Among these are mentioned, by name, the governor of one State (Indiana), and many judges and members of Congress as having risen from the condition of labouring men.

Others, again, quote their own lives and fortunes as instances of this progress, valuing their properties in some instances as high as $50,000 (ten thousand guineas). Here is the table of average farm wages for the last five years. It is to be noted, that, 1. Wages and cost of board are this year one-fifth higher than this average. 2. That the employer provides board and lodging, and generally washing and mending, in addition to these wages. 3. That "summer months" means six or eight active farm months. The variations in amount in the same locality depend on variations in demand and on the skill of the workman. The names of States are represented by their initial letters only, from want of space.

LOCALITY. State and County.	In summer by the month.	In harvest by the day.	In harvest by the month.	For the whole year.	Cost of board per week.
Maine, Somerset	$12	$	$	$	$1 75
	15				
Mass., Franklin			26		
	15	1 25	30	150	1 50
Do., Hampshire ..			420		1 25
Con., New-haven		1 25	32		
	20	1 50	39	180	2 00
Do., New-haven		1 25	32		
	20	1 50	39	180	2 00
Do., New-haven ..	13	1 25	20	125	1 75
Do., Fairfield ..	10	1 00	11	120	
	14	1 25	16	150	2 25
Do., Hartford ..			20	120	1 75
	15	1 50	25	150	2 50
Do., Middlesex	12	1 00	15	120	2 59
	18	1 50	20	180	2 00
Do., Litchfield ..	14	1 25	20	126	2 90
N. Y., Madison			26	120	
	15		30	144	1 50
Do., Wayne ..	10		16	100	
	16		24	120	2 00
N. Y., Ontario			25	120	
		1 50	30	160	1 50
Do., Madison		1 00	20		1 50
Do., Onondaga	10	1 00	15	100	
	15	1 25	25	125	2 00
Do., Oneida....		1 00			
	14	1 25	20	150	2 00
Do., Otsego		1 00	22	144	1 50
Do., Columbia ..	12	1 00	24	85	1 00
Do., Columbia	10		20		1 50
	16	1 25	25	150	1 75
Do., Dutchess	15	1 25	26	150	2 00
	12	1 25			1 25
Do., Oswego ..	14	1 50	20	110	1 75
Do., Dutchess	16		20	130	
	18	1 25	24	144	
Do., Sullivan	14	1 25	18	140	2 00
Do., Seneca ..	13	87		120	1 50
	15	1 50	18	150	1 75
Do., Dutchess ..	15	1 25	15	165	2 25

LOCALITY. State and County.	In summer by the month.	In harvest by the day.	In harvest by the month.	For the whole year.	Cost of board per week.
N. Y., Columbia	$15	$1 50	$25	160	$2 50
Do., Onondaga	12	1 00			
	13	1 25	20	120	2 00
Do., Richmond	10	1 25	14		1 50
	13	1 50	20	108	2 50
Do., Erie & Niagara	12	1 00	20		
	15	1 50	24	144	2 00
Do., Oneida....					1 50
	12	1 00			2 00
Do. Montgomery	10	87	15	100	
	12	1 00	20	130	1 75
Do., Herkimer	12	75	15	120	
	14	1 50	18	140	
Do., Livingston		1 00		120	
		1 25	25	140	1 00
N. J., Salem ..			13	125	1 50
	12	1 06	14	130	1 75
Do., Monmouth		1 00		100	2 00
		1 50		120	2 50
Do., Gloucester ..	12	1 25	16	120	1 75
	14				
Penn., Crawford	15	75		120	
Do., Susquehanna	14	1	16	144	1 50
	14			115	
Do., Bucks	16	1 75	20	150	2 00
	16	1	20	144	1 50
Do., Bradford					1 75
	18	1 25	20	150	2 00
Do., Lancaster	11				
	12	1 00	15	120	1 50
Do., do.	10	75	13	90	1 75
Do., Ferguson....					1 00
Do., Perry	10	75	13	96	1 25
				20	
Md. Prince Geo.		1 50		100	
Do., Washington	10	1 00			1 12
	11	2 00		115	1 25
Do., do.		1 25			
	12	2 00		120	2 00
Va., Washington	10	75		100	1 50
	13	1 00	13	120	2 00
S. C., Anderson					1 50
	15	1 00	25	120	2 00

LOCALITY. State and County.	WAGES. (Board found by employer.) When hired. In summer by the month.	In harvest by the day.	In harvest by the month.	For the whole year.	Cost of board per week.
Northern Mississippi	$	$	$ 12	120 (cl.)	$
				15 (cl.)	
Texas, Bexar ..	20	2 00		150	2 00
	25			225	3 00
				100	
Ky. Clark (sl.)		1 00		(cl.)	2 50
Mo., St. Joseph's	12	1 00		120	
	15	1 25	25	175	2 00
Ohio, Cohocton				110	
		1 00		120	2 00
Ohio, Belmont		1 00	20	100	
		1 50	30	125	1 50
Do., Ashtabula		1 00			
	13	1 50	25		1 50
Do., Highland	12			120	
	16			150	
Do., Dark		1 00	18	125	1 50
Do., Mahoming ..	18	75		130	1 25
Do., Crawford		75		125	1 75
	15	1 00		150	2 00
Mich., Branch ..	13	1 25	22	144	1 50
Do., Cass	18	1 50		200	1 75
	25			230	
Do., Battle creek	12	75		140	
	15	1 50		180	
Ind., Gibson	14	1 25	18	120	1 50
Do., Greencastle	15	1 00		144	1 50
	18	1 50		180	2 00
Do., Delaware ..	13	1 00	20	120	1 50
Do., Harrison....	10	1 00	18	96	1 50
Do.. Stuben·	12	1 00	20	120	1 75
Ill., Lake	15	1 25	20	125	1 75

LOCALITY. State and County.	WAGES. (Board found by employer.) When hired. In summer by the month.	In harvest by the day.	In harvest by the month.	For the whole year.	Cost of board per week.
Ill., Newark ..	$ 13	$1 00	$ 18	130	$1 50
	15	1 50	24	150	2 00
Do., Pike	13	1 00		144	
Do., Will......	12			100	1 50
	15			150	
Do., Tazewell		1 00	23	150	2 00
Do., Stephenson	12	1 00		120	
	16	2 00		150	1 50
Do., Bureau ..		1 50		180	
	25	2 00	30	220	2 00
Do., Winnebago				100	
	15			150	
Do., Whiteside	15	1 25		100	1 00
	18	1 50	25	120	1 50
Do. Marshall ..	15	1 25	25	165	1 25
	16				1 50
Do., Ogle	12			160	
	13				
Do., Hancock..				125	1 50
	14	1 00	22	150	2 00
Do., Winnebago..	13	1 12	18	130	1 50
Do., Will......		75	20	140	1 50
		1 50	30	200	2 50
Do., Pulaski	15	1 00		120	1 50
Iowa., Lee	12	1 00		120	1 50
Do., Keokuk ..				120	
				240	
Wis., Fond du Lac	14	1 12	20	140	1 25
Do., Walworth		1 00	18	100	
	12	1 50	20	150	1 50
Do., Kenosha ..	13				1 50
	12	1 50	24	144	2 25

The following are some questions and replies not already alluded to above :—

Q. Could more labourers find employment steadily and permanently at the rate of wages you have mentioned? A. Eighty-eight reply—9 say No; 3 say "In summer;" 76 say YES—17 with great emphasis and urgency. [The Noes come from New England, and the immediate vicinity of New York and Philadelphia.]

Q. (1.) Is it a frequent, occasional, or extremely rare occurrence for men who have been employed as hired hands upon farms, within your observation, to come upon the public for support of life, or to be dependent in any way upon charity? (2.) Does this ever happen to men of sound body and not of intemperate habits? A. Of eighty-four who reply, 80 say "Very rarely" or "Never;" 2 (in New York and New Jersey) say "Occasional;" 2 (in Massachusetts and Maryland) say "Frequent." To the second question—1 (Massachusetts) says "Yes;" 2 say "Very rarely;" 79 say "No."

Q. Do the majority of labourers take their meals at the same table with their employers? A. It appears to be the almost universal custom for labourer and employer to sit at the same family table—not excepting the female "help." Two employers only, living near New York city, say "No." The eighty-six others all reply affirmatively, some with pride, some even with indignation.

Q. Have they as much food as they wish to eat? A. Two pass this question in silence; 86 reply "Of course," of whom one adds, "*Our dogs have food to spare.*"

Q. Are they generally decently and comfortably clothed? A. Eighty-two say "Yes;" one says, With few exceptions; many agree in mentioning that they are *as well* clothed as their employers, and, not without pique, some add "*better.*"

The demand for FEMALES appears to be everywhere even greater and more uniform than that for males. To *sixty-eight* of these letters are added remarks on female labour, and the general expression is, that they are very scarce and "*in great demand.*" *Only one* reports that in his region (near Utica, N. Y.) the supply is about equal to the demand. One says, "One hundred could find employers in this town in one day." The wages reported are from 75 cents to $2 a week, varying according to experience and capacity. Many, especially at the West, report the customary position of such girls in the family as that of daughters, sitting at the same table, dressing as well or better, riding to the village to church in the same vehicle, and say that they appear to marry even quicker than the ladies. The tendency throughout the West to *immediate marriage* is a subject of general complaint. One counts over his girls on his fingers with this curious statistical result: "In the last eight years I have had in my employ 23 girls, 19 of whom have married out of my house."

On the whole, the result of his inquiry seems to demonstrate what of late has here (in New York city) been this winter considered doubtful, namely, that *the demand for agricultural and household labour still exists in full force*, and is almost limitless in extent. Labourers of one year are the employers of the next, increasing by so much more the constant demand, and exhausting the stream of supply.

From A. C. Buchanan, Chief Gov! Emigration Agent, Quebec, to V. F., Aug. 4, 1854: "If your brother or any other gentleman will only manage to get their surplus labourers out to this country, I will undertake to provide them all with employment. I have never known such a season as this, and the universal complaint from one end of the country to the other is of the impossibility of securing labourers. Scarcely a post arrives that does not bring me an application from parties requesting me to send them labourers and mechanics, and they will guarantee them steady profitable employment." The same writer reports to the British Government, that of a party of 44 girls forwarded to him during the month of August, the whole were engaged the day after their arrival; and that if ten times their number were landed in the morning, they could be similarly disposed of before sundown.

From Captain Fuller, residing at Simcoe, near London, Canada West, to the Chief Government Emigration Agent at Quebec, Aug. 9, 1854: ". . . If the importation from any one union does not exceed 250, I will provide for the whole of them within a circle of five miles. Nearly every one of those sent me before (230) are within that range now, except a few that have married, and two gone to New York. . . . There is not, as you are aware, a finer portion of the province than this county (Norfolk): *Labourers, labourers,* and domestic *servants, servants*—servants is the one great cry, the great want of the country. I see several parties noticed in the papers as still expected to arrive; do pray contrive to send me one whole cargo." [I saw Captain Fuller and many of the girls whom he had placed.—V. F.]

From the Mayor of Port Hope, a small town east of Toronto, in West Canada, to the Government Emigration Agent at Montreal, Sept. 6, 1854: "I have to acknowledge the receipt of your favour of the 2nd inst., inclosing a list of fifty-four young women forwarded by you to this place in quest of employment. The young women in question arrived here yesterday, and I am happy to inform you that, during the course of the day, thirty-five of them found employment in good situations, and at the wages they demanded. I find this evening that only six remain unemployed, three or four of whom are under medical treatment for some slight indisposition, and I have no doubt that all will be disposed of by to-morrow evening. In the meantime they have been provided with food and quarters by the order of the municipal council of the town. I have to return you many thanks for your prompt compliance with the request I addressed to the Chief Emigration Agent on this subject, by which a serious inconvenience, under which many of my fellow-townsmen were suffering, has been removed. [In Ireland it is the poor girls who suffer the *serious inconvenience.*—V. F.] I may at the same time remark, that immediate and permanent employment at a high rate of wages can be found here for a large body of able-bodied men on the railway and harbour now in course of construction, on both of which serious complaints are made of the scarcity and difficulty in procuring labourers. I presume that 400 or 500 persons might be provided with employment if you could forward that number to this place. . . ."

New laws for the regulation of passenger ships are proposed to be passed in America and England. The principal new provisions of the former are, 1. More space for each passenger below and on deck; 2, more food to be issued, cooked, between specified hours; 3, the passage money of those who die on the voyage to be returned to their relations or to an emigrant's poorhouse. The British bill contains similar provisions, except the last, and besides requires waterclosets below for female passengers when there are fifty, and that passengers shall receive 1s. 6d. a day detention money instead of 1s. The great quantity of provisions required by the British bill is, I think, quite unnecessary, and simply calculated to make emigration difficult for the poor. 2 lbs. more flour and a pint of peas or beans per week, and 1 lb of meat, was, I believe, all the extra quantity required.

Printed for W. & F. G. Cash, 5, Bishopsgate Street Without, London.

AS I AM.

IRISH FEMALE EMIGRATION.

For the purpose of raising the condition of the poorest families in the poorest districts of Ireland, by assisting the emigration of one female member of each family, specially selected on account of her poverty, good character, and industrious habits, with the expectation that she will herself take the remaining members of her family out of poverty.

No. of Subscribers March 1, 1855......1000.

Amount subscribed......£55 0 0.

I sent 105 persons from County Clare, Ireland, with the proceeds of a similar fund, raised nearly three years ago. I have received no bad accounts of any of them, and most of them have already sent for other members of their families, some for as many as five and six. **V. F.**

Those of my readers who approve of the above proposal are respectfully requested to collect subscriptions of from one penny upwards in aid, and to remit the amount in postage stamps or post office order, for me to the care of my publishers, Messrs. W. & F. G. CASH, Bishopsgate, London, or pay it to my account with my bankers, Messrs. COUTTS, Strand, London.

Those who can afford 10s. or 15s. more can have more privacy on ship-board, and for other 10s. or 15s. can have their meals cooked by the Captain's cook.

[SEE COVER AT COMMENCEMENT.]

Area and Population of the United States in 1790 and 1850.

Names of States.	Square Miles.	Population in 1790.	Total Pop. in 1850.	Pop. to sq. m.
Maine	32,854	96,540	583,169	19
New Hampshire	9,280	141,899	317,976	34
Vermont	10,212	85,416	314,120	30
Massachusetts	7,800	378,717	994,514	126
Rhode Island	1,306	69,110	147,545	108
Connecticut	4,674	238,141	370,792	79
New York	47,000	340,120	3,097,394	65
New Jersey	8,320	184,139	489,555	60
Pennsylvania	46,000	434,373	2,311,786	50
Delaware	2,120	59,098	91,532	44
Maryland	9,356	319,728	583,034	62
District of Columbia	60	....	51,687	861
Virginia	61,352	748,308	1,421,661	23
North Carolina	50,000	393,751	869,039	17
South Carolina	29,000	249,073	668,507	23
Georgia	58,000	82,548	906,185	16
Florida	59,268	....	87,445	$1\frac{1}{2}$
Alabama	50,722	....	771,623	15
Mississippi	47,156	....	606,526	13
Louisiana	46,431	....	517,762	11
Texas	237,321	....	212,592	1
Arkansas	52,198	....	209,897	4
Tennessee	45,600	30,791	1,002,717	23
Kentucky	37,680	73,077	982,405	26
Ohio	39,964	....	1,980,329	50
Michigan	56,243	....	397,654	7
Indiana	33,809	....	988,416	29
Illinois	55,405	....	851,470	15
Missouri	67,380	....	682,044	10
Iowa	50,914	....	192,214	4
Wisconsin	53,924	....	305,391	6
California	188,981	....	92,597	1
Minnesota	166,000	....	6,077	1 to 28
Oregon, inc. Washington Ter.	341,463	....	13,294	1 to 25
Utah	187,923	....	11,380	1 to 16
New Mexico	257,744	....	61,547	1 to 4
Nebraska and Kansas	482,000	....	....	..
Indian Territory	68,000	....	....	..
Total	3,033,460	3,929,872	23,191,876	8

Distances by Rail and Steam Boat on the most direct routes from New York.

	Miles.		Miles.		Miles.
Albany, N. Y.	143	Galena, Ill.	1291	Madison, Wis.	1400
Alton, Ill.	1415	Green Bay, Wis.	1400	Milwaukee, Wis.	1445
Baltimore, Md.	210	Hamilton, Ca.	605	Monroe, Mich.	814
Buffalo, N. Y.	504	Indianapolis, Ind.	1140	Montreal, Ca.	375
Burlington, Iowa	1650	Iowa City, Iowa	1700	Narrowsburgh, N.Y.	122
Chicago, Ill.	1131	Joliet, Ill.	1170	Nauvoo, Ill.	1800
Cincinnati, O.	959	Kenosha, Wis.	1509	Niagara Falls, N. Y.	524
Cleveland, O.	704	Kingston, Ca.	600	Ogdensburgh, N. Y.	460
Columbus, O.	936	Lafayette, Ind.	1036	Parkersburgh, Va.	890
Detroit, Mich.	850	Lasalle, Ill.	1200	Peoria, Ill.	1270
Dubuque, Iowa	1310	Louisville, Ky.	1089	Philadelphia, Pa.	90
Dunkirk, N. Y.	469	Mackinaw, Mich.	1114	Pittsburgh, Pa.	482

RECORD OF TREATMENT, EXTRACTION ETC.

Shelfmark: **8276. b. 4.**

S&P Ref No. **2x2/80.**

Microfilm No.

Date	Particulars	
	pH Before or Existing	pH After
Sept. 1999	6.85	6.85

Deacidification

Adhesives

Wheat starch Paste.
Animal Gel. Glue (BIND)

Lined / Laminated

Chemicals / Solvents

Cover Treatment

Other Remarks

9 781535 816113